The Ottoman-Russian Wars of the 19th Century: The History of the Conflicts Between Russia and the Ottoman Empire Leading Up to World War I

By Charles River Editors

A painting of the Siege of Sevastopol during the Crimean War

Introduction

A painting of the Russian siege of Varna during the Crimean War

In terms of geopolitics, perhaps the most seminal event of the Middle Ages was the successful Ottoman siege of Constantinople in 1453. The city had been an imperial capital as far back as the 4th century, when Constantine the Great shifted the power center of the Roman Empire there, effectively establishing two almost equally powerful halves of antiquity's greatest empire. Constantinople would continue to serve as the capital of the Byzantine Empire even after the Western half of the Roman Empire collapsed in the late 5th century. Naturally, the Ottoman Empire would also use Constantinople as the capital of its empire after their conquest effectively ended the Byzantine Empire, and thanks to its strategic location, it has been a trading center for years and remains one today under the Turkish name of Istanbul.

The end of the Byzantine Empire had a profound effect not only on the Middle East but Europe as well. Constantinople had played a crucial part in the Crusades, and the fall of the Byzantines meant that the Ottomans now shared a border with Europe. The Islamic empire was viewed as a threat by the predominantly Christian continent to their west, and it took little time for different European nations to start clashing with the powerful Turks. In fact, the Ottomans would clash with Russians, Austrians, Venetians, Polish, and more before collapsing as a result of World War I, when they were part of the Central powers.

The Ottoman conquest of Constantinople also played a decisive role in fostering the Renaissance in Western Europe. The Byzantine Empire's influence had helped ensure that it was the custodian of various ancient texts, most notably from the ancient Greeks, and when Constantinople fell, Byzantine refugees flocked west to seek refuge in Europe. Those refugees brought books that helped spark an interest in antiquity that fueled the Italian Renaissance and essentially put an end to the Middle Ages altogether.

In the wake of taking Constantinople, the Ottoman Empire would spend the next few centuries expanding its size, power, and influence, bumping up against Eastern Europe and becoming one of the world's most important geopolitical players. It was a rise that would not truly start to wane until the 19th century, and in the centuries before the decline of the "sick man of Europe," the Ottomans frequently tried to push further into Europe.

Some of those forays were memorably countered by Western Europeans and the Holy League, but the Ottomans' most frequent foe was the Russian Empire, which opposed them for both geopolitical and religious reasons. From negotiations to battles, the two sides jockeyed for position over the course of hundreds of years, and the start of the fighting may have represented the Ottomans' best chance to conquer Moscow and change the course of history.

By the 19th century, the tsar was notoriously referring to the Ottoman Empire as the "sick man of Europe," and by the start of World War I, the Ottoman Empire was often described as a dwindling power, mired by administrative corruption, using inferior technology, and plagued by poor leadership. The general idea is that the Ottoman Empire was "lagging behind," likely coming from the clear stagnation of the empire between 1683 and 1826. Yet it can be argued that this portrayal is often misleading and fails to give a fuller picture of the state of the Ottoman Empire. The fact that the other existing multicultural empire, the Austro-Hungarian Empire, also did not survive World War I should put into question this "accepted narrative." Looking at the reforms, technological advances and modernization efforts made by the Ottoman elite between 1826 and the beginning of World War I, one could really wonder why such a thirst for change failed to save the Ottomans when similar measures taken by other nations, such as Japan during the Meiji era, did in fact result in the rise of a global power in the 20th century.

During the period that preceded its collapse, the Ottoman Empire was at the heart of a growing rivalry between two of the competing global powers of the time, England and France. The two powers asserted their influence over a declining empire, the history of which is anchored in Europe as much as in Asia. However, while the two powers were instrumental in the final defeat and collapse of the Ottoman Empire, their stance toward what came to be known as the "Eastern Question" – the fate of the Ottoman Empire – is not one of clear enmity. Both England and France found, at times, reasons to extend the life of the sick man of Europe until it finally sided with their shared enemies. Russia's stance toward the Ottoman Empire is much more clear-cut; the rising Asian and European powers saw the Ottomans as a rival, which they strove to contain, divide, and finally destroy for more than 300 years in a series of wars against their old adversary.

The Ottoman-Russian Wars of the 19th Century: The History of the Conflicts Between Russia and the Ottoman Empire Leading Up to World War I looks at the various origins of the belligerence, how the battles went, and how they influenced both empires' histories. Along with pictures of important people and places, you will learn about the 19th century wars like never before.

The Ottoman-Russian Wars of the 19th Century: The History of the Conflicts Between Russia and the Ottoman Empire Leading Up to World War I

About Charles River Editors

Introduction

The Ottomans and Russians

The Dawn of the 19th Century

The Greek Revolution and the War of 1829-30

The Crimean War

The War of 1877-1878

Prelude to World War I

The Legacy of the Ottoman-Russian Wars

Online Resources

Further Reading

Free Books by Charles River Editors

Discounted Books by Charles River Editors

The Ottomans and Russians

The Ottoman Empire is often referred to as the Turkish Empire by people today and its contemporaries, but the name is something of a misnomer. Though Turkish was the language of the state, the Turks made up a small portion of the empire for most of its history.[1] The Ottoman state was a truly multiethnic entity based on allegiance to the head of the tribe of *Osman* ("Ottoman" in archaic English). Toward the end of the 16th century - the time when the Russians and Ottomans first clashed - the Sultan of "the Sublime Ottoman State"[2] was the absolute ruler of an empire encompassing Anatolia, the Balkans, the northern coasts of the Black Sea, Syria, Mesopotamia, Palestine, Arabia, Egypt, and northern Africa to Morocco. Moreover, the Ottoman fleet dominated the Western Mediterranean and raided extensively as far as England, Ireland, and the shipping lanes of the Indian Ocean.

The mighty edifice that was the Ottoman Empire rested on three pillars: the Sultan, Islam, and *jihad*. The Ottoman state was considered an extension of the Sultan's household, and as such, he ruled as an absolute monarch. He was the *padishah* (emperor), commander of the faithful and caliph, and the shadow of God on Earth, and as such, representative and ruler of the entire world. All the world was bound to submit to Allah, and thus, to his representative. That was not to say that his rule was arbitrary; quite the contrary. He was bound by the prescriptions of Islamic law and might even be deposed with the approval of the *ulema* - a college of Islamic jurists - if he failed to protect them. The administration of justice was considered one of the Sultan's highest duties, the other being the protection and advancement of the Islamic faith. According to Islamic scholars, the Quran commanded holy war, jihad, which was aimed not at the conversion of non-Muslims, but the expansion of the Islamic state.[3] In this respect, it was distinct from the medieval Christian concept of the crusade, which was (on paper at least) a purely defensive war. In theory, the state of war would last until the entire world had fallen under Islamic rule, though in practice, temporary truces were permitted.[4]

Islamic armies were permitted to despoil unbelievers and enslave them, and goods and slaves taken in war were important elements of the Ottoman economy. The Sultan relied upon them both for his personal status and the enrichment of the soldiers upon which the empire relied. The famous Janissaries were slave-soldiers of the Sultan, taken as boys from Christian families under Ottoman rule. Under a form of human taxation called *devshirme,* government officers selected boys aged between six and 14 every five years who were raised as Muslims and trained, either as Janissaries or for government service. These youths were cared for and paid generously by the Sultan, and they owed their often prestigious positions to him. The post of grand vizier, the most powerful in the empire beneath the Sultan, was filled mostly by European - often Albanian -

---

[1] "Turk" was actually a term of disparagement, for a Turk was usually an Anatolian peasant, viewed without education or sophistication (Ágoston, 2009, p. xxvi).

[2] Özgündenli, 2005

[3] Peters, 2009, p. 3

[4] Lews, 1993, pp. 9-10

slaves. The Sultan, therefore, had a power base independent of the free Ottoman nobility. The Sultan also took his wives from a harem of slaves, avoiding the political strife so often associated with marriage alliances in the aristocracy.

The Sultan did not rely solely on slaves for his military. Indeed, the backbone of the Ottoman Army was the *sipahi*, free elite cavalrymen. Sipahis were granted fiefs by the monarch in return for keeping a certain number of cavalry and auxiliary troops in peak condition for the military. They were, in this respect, equivalent to the western European knight, except they did not own their land and had no right to pass it on to their heirs. This prevented the rise of local aristocracies that might challenge the imperial government. A sipahi's grant or *timar* was usually taken from conquered territories, and this, on top of the religious imperative to jihad and the need for slave labor, necessitated a continuous state of war.

The Ottoman military was noted for its mastery of musketry and gunpowder artillery, employed effectively at a time when many western armies were still coming to terms with them. Massive bombards were instrumental in bringing down Constantinople, the last stronghold of the Roman[5] (Byzantine) Empire in 1453. The Ottomans were also excellent engineers and sappers, and their ability to mine under walls to bring them down was especially feared.

Despite the bellicose nature of the empire, the Ottomans fostered education, scholarship, literature, art, and architecture, though within the theological boundaries of Islam, as interpreted by the *ulema*. The Sultans and members of the imperial family were highly educated, and they were expected to be proficient in the higher arts, such as poetry and calligraphy.

Life for a non-Muslim subject of the Ottoman Sultan was not generally oppressive. Christians and Jews were called "People of the Book" in the Quran, and as such, were entitled to legal protection. They were permitted to practice their religions without coercion but were forbidden to proselytize. Furthermore, they continued to be governed by their own laws as long as they did not violate the rights of Muslims and the Sultan and as long as they paid taxes. These taxes, however, were higher than those imposed upon Muslims, and this proved an incentive for many to convert to Islam, which also gave them the opportunity to advance their careers. Non-Muslim jurisdictions were referred to as *millets* (nations) and were usually governed by the highest-ranking dignity. For example, the political head of the Roman Millet (*millet-i Rûm*) was the Ecumenical Patriarch of Constantinople. Besides heavier taxes, Christian millets also beared the burden of the devsirme (Jews were exempt).

The great military successes of the Ottoman Empire during the 15th and 16th centuries are to be attributed in no small part to the military's organization, training, and efficiency. The Sultans were able to raise large numbers of troops in a relatively short time. The political structure of the

---

[5] The state often referred to as the Byzantine Empire was, in fact, a direct continuation of the East Roman Empire. After the conquest of Constantinople, the Sultans continued to refer to their Greek subjects as Romans and themselves as *Qayser-i Rûm* ("Caesar of Rome") (David, 2000, p. 85).

empire, based on trained slaves dependent directly upon the Sultan, minimized the political instability that so often hampered military activity in Christian Europe. The national interests of the states of central and Eastern Europe, as well as the intrigue of the feudal nobility within those states, hindered effective resistance. The infamous fall of Hungary to the Ottomans at the Battle of Mohacs (1526) was due as much to internal dissension as the might of the Ottoman military, and it brought the Sultan's armies to the Danube, in sight of the German city of Vienna. The Ottomans actually laid siege to the city in 1529, but they were repelled by the tenacity of the troops of the Imperial House of Habsburg, though more by the inclement weather that rendered its artillery useless.

To the west, the Ottomans took to the seas to gain supremacy in the Eastern Mediterranean. Their attempts to conquer the western sea were checked by their failure to capture Malta in 1566 and the great naval battle of Lepanto in the Bay of Corinth in 1571. The Ottomans never again attempted to rule the whole of the Mediterranean, though pirates regularly raided the shores of Italy, France, and Spain for slaves and booty, and they continued to do so until the beginning of the 19th century. On land, however, the Ottoman military in the Balkans remained unconquered, though the Habsburgs and their allies were, for the time being, able to limit further Ottoman expansion.

In many respects, the origins of the conflict between the Ottoman Empire and Russia revolved around the Black Sea coast around the Volga in what is now Ukraine as well as the Khanate of Crimea. The latter, which extended from Moldavia to the Sea of Azov, was a remnant of the Great Golden Horde, which settled in the Russian Steppes in the thirteenth century and conquered Russian principalities. Over the course of the fourteenth century, the Horde declined and fragmented to the beginning of the fifteenth. The largest and most powerful of the successor states was the Crimean Khanate, ruled by a direct descendant of Genghis Khan, with his capital at Bahçeseray, about 40 kilometers northeast of Sevastopol. The inhabitants of Crimea, as of the whole of the Steppes, were Tatars, a Turco-Mongolian people. They were often called tartars in the West, a play on words since *Tartarus* was a word used for hell, and the terror inflicted by the Turco-Mongolian hordes was legendary.

Crimean Tatars relied on the slave trade for their prosperity, raiding Muscovy, Poland, and Lithuania for captives and selling them in Genoese (later Ottoman) ports on the Crimean Peninsula, such as Kherson and Caffa (Feodosia). It is estimated that during the 16th and 17th centuries, as many as 2,000,000 slaves were exported from these ports, and in 1669, a single raid into Russia brought back 20,000 captives.

The Ottoman Empire, dependent upon a constant supply of slaves, naturally coveted the khanate and its trade, and in 1475, they conquered the Christian Genoese ports and forced the Khan of Crimea to accept Ottoman suzerainty. In effect, the khanate continued as an independent nation, though succession depended on the approval of the Sultan until 1524, when the Sultans directly appointed the Khan. With control of the Black Sea in Ottoman hands, the Sultans now had a direct interest in protecting the Crimean khanate and weakening Russia.

Russia, once a great empire extending from the Baltic to the Black Sea, was much weakened by the time the Golden Horde invaded in the 13th century. The grand prince of Kiev was nominally lord of all the "land of the Rus," but in reality, it was a collection of warring principalities. The Golden Horde kept up the pretense of appointing a grand prince who collected tribute for the Great Khan, and it encouraged the continued rivalries between the principalities.

At the time of the Mongol invasion (1238), the town of Moscow was a trading post of no great importance within the principality of Vladimir-Suzdal. Over the next 80 years, ambitious princes expanded their territories by conquering their neighbors and currying favor with the Great Khan until, in 1318, Prince Yuri (George) Danilovich was appointed grand prince of all the Rus. In time, Muscovy became powerful enough to challenge its Tatar overlords, and in 1476, Grand Prince Ivan III successfully stopped paying tribute to the Horde, which was rapidly fragmenting into rival dynasties. He then proceeded to unite all of the Russian principalities under his rule, a task which he completed by the time of his death in 1505.

It should be noted that the Russia of Ivan III, though vast, comprised only a portion of the nation now known as the Russian Federation. It stretched east to the Ural Mountains, north to the border of Swedish Finland, and south to the Upper Volga region. The Tatar states, successors to the Golden Horde in the Steppes, were no longer a serious threat to the Russians, but nevertheless, remained formidable. To the west, southern Russia, the land of the former principality of Kiev was ruled by Catholic Lithuania (in a personal union with Poland) and called Ruthenia. Likewise, White Russia (Belarus) was governed by Lithuania. Livonia, roughly corresponding to modern Latvia and Estonia, was also Catholic. Muscovy was devoutly Orthodox, and when the Roman Catholics and Eastern Orthodox Christians split in the 11th century, the Rus stood firmly with Constantinople, the spiritual and political head of Eastern Orthodox Christianity.

The foreign policy of grand princes after Ivan III was governed by three imperatives: 1) to regain Ruthenia from the western Catholics and fully restore the unity of the Russian state; 2) to gain a major port in the Baltic; and 3) to gain a warm water port on the Black Sea which would allow it to trade overseas year-round (the ports on the Baltic and Barents Sea were ice-bound for much of the year). The last necessarily brought Muscovy into conflict with the Khanate of Crimea and its master, the Ottoman Empire.

In several respects, the Grand Principality of Muscovy and the Ottoman Empire were similar. Both were absolute monarchies, and the ruler of Muscovy owned the greater portion of land in his dominions, so there was no legislative body to check his power. There was an established noble class, the *boyars*, but the conquests of the Muscovite prince had severely diminished their capacity to share power with the monarch. Nevertheless, the prince relied upon them for his military, and as the Ottoman Sultan granted *timars* in return for military service, so the Muscovite monarch gave the boyars land with the expectation they would maintain a certain number of cavalry.

Like the Ottoman Empire, Muscovy also depended upon slavery. Various laws enacted throughout the 15th and 16th centuries increasingly bound peasants to the boyars' estates, ensuring a regular source of labor and taxation. In the 16th century, the practice of selling these serfs had not yet become commonplace, but still, the distinction between slavery and serfdom was so little as to be inconsequential.

The Ottoman Empire and Muscovy were also similar in their connection to Constantinople, the former seat of the Eastern Roman Empire and then the Byzantine Empire. The city was the capital of the Sultans, who regarded themselves as the successors of the Roman emperors and styled themselves as *Qayser-i Rûm* ("Caesar of Rome").[6] Similarly, the grand princes of Muscovy also came to see themselves as successors of the Roman emperor, using the title of *Tsar* ("Caesar"). When Constantinople fell to the Ottomans in 1453, Muscovy's rulers saw themselves as the sole bastions of Christian Orthodoxy and defenders of the faith, a role assumed by subsequent Russian emperors. Grand Prince Ivan III was also married to Sophia Palaiologina, daughter of Constantine XI, the last Byzantine emperor.

In 1547, Ivan IV (The Terrible), grandson of Sophia, first assumed the title "Tsar of All Rus," though Ivan III had used the title informally. Moscow came to be referred to as the "Third Rome," the other two being Rome and Constantinople. In a letter to Ivan III, Monk Filofey of Pskov wrote, "I would like to say a few words about the existing [o]rthodox empire of our most illustrious…exalted ruler. He is the only emperor on all the earth over the Christians, the governor of the holy, divine throne of the holy, ecumenical, apostolic [C]hurch, which, in place of the churches of Rome and Constantinople, is in the city of Moscow, protected by God…in the holy and glorious Uspenskij Church of the most pure Mother of God. It alone shines over all the earth more radiantly than the sun. For know well, those who love Christ and those who love God, that all Christian empires will perish and give way to the one kingdom of our ruler…in accord with the books of the [P]rophet, which is the Russian [E]mpire. For two Romes have fallen, but the third stands, and there will never be a fourth."[7]

As the Ottoman emperor was legitimized as the earthly representative of Allah and leader of perpetual jihad, so the Muscovite ruler was sanctified by his succession to the throne of the Christian Roman emperor. As such, he believed he not only had the right but the responsibility to liberate the Orthodox under the tyranny of both Catholic and Islamic rule. This concept remains today, as noted by Metropolitan Hilarion of New York in 2013: "As sons and daughters of the Russian Orthodox Church, we are all citizens of Holy Russia. When we speak of Holy Russia,

---

[6] See note 5.
[7] van den Bercken, 1999, p. 146

we are not talking about the Russian Federation or any civil society on earth; rather, it is a way of life that has been passed down to us through the centuries by such great saints of the Russian Land as the Holy Great Prince Vladimir and Great Princess Olga, Venerable Sergius of Radonezh, Job of Pochaev, Seraphim of Sarov, and more recently, the countless New Martyrs and Confessors of the 20th [sic] century. These saints are our ancestors, and we must look to them for instruction on how to bravely confess the Faith [sic], even when facing persecution. There is no achievement in simply calling oneself "Russian": in order to be a genuine Russian, one must first become [o]rthodox and live a life in the Church, as did our forebears, the founders of Holy Russia!"[8]

Given that both the Ottoman Empire and Muscovy believed their rulers had the absolute right to rule and possessed a divine mandate to expand their borders, in terms of geopolitics and ideology, the empires were bound to clash.

The Khanate of Astrakhan was one of the successor states of the Golden Horde and arguably the most important, commanding the exit of the Volga into the Caspian Sea and with it the most important trading route through Russia. Astrakhan was the largest slave market on the Volga, making it of importance to the Ottoman Empire. It was also of importance to the Muscovite Empire.

After defeating the Astrakhan Tatars in a battle outside the city in 1554, Tsar Ivan IV imposed a puppet ruler, Dervish Ali, who quickly rebelled and invited the Ottomans into the khanate. However, Ottoman intervention could not prevent the fall of Astrakhan to the Muscovite prince, who proclaimed himself Tsar of Astrakhan two years later. The Tsar quickly refortified the city and ended its lucrative slave markets.

---

[8] Hilarion, 2013

A portrait of Ivan IV

In Constantinople, the fall of Astrakhan was met with more annoyance than outrage. Grand Vizier of Sultan Selim II Sokollu Mehmet conceived a plan of building a canal connecting the Volga to the Don, which flowed into the Sea of Azov and would have connected the Astrakhan slave trade with that of Crimea. Had it been realized, it would have been a monumental engineering enterprise, for the shortest distance between the rivers is more than 450 kilometers. A canal would also have allowed for the speedy transportation of troops, which some historians suggest were aimed at Central Asia and Persia rather than Russia.[9] The Vizier was more than confident that the plan was still realizable, but it required a major military campaign.

---

[9] Barudel, 1995, p. 1059

Sokollu Mehmet Pasha

After securing Selim's consent, Sokollu Mehmet dispatched 20,000 troops, joined by 30,000-50,000 Crimean cavalry to conquer Astrakhan, using the fortress of Azov at the mouth of the Don as a base. The combined force appeared before the walls of Astrakhan in the summer of 1569 and laid siege to it. At the same time, a vast number of slaves from Moldavia and Wallachia (now Romania) began work on the canal. A vigorous sortie led by Pyotr Serebrianyi, the governor of the city, succeeded in driving back the besieging army, commanded by Kasim Pasha and Khan Devlet I Giray of Crimea, long enough to allow time for the relief force from Moscow to arrive. The latter crushed Kasim's force and the terrified canal laborers fled for their lives. The Ottoman fleet was destroyed in a storm in the Sea of Azov, meaning that the shattered remnants of the Ottoman-Tatar Army were trapped on the Steppes. Most froze to death in the savage autumn cold or fell victim to Circassian raiders from the Caucasus. Sokullo might have replaced his army with no great difficulty, but rebuilding the Black Sea fleet took considerable time and resources. Therefore, the Ottomans agreed to sign the Treaty of Constantinople with the Russians in 1570. The peace affirmed the Muscovite possession of Astrakhan and guaranteed the freedom of Ottoman pilgrims and traders.

A depiction of Khan Devlet I Giray

The defeat rankled, however, and Khan Devlet I Giray plotted revenge with his Ottoman masters. By May 1571, he had massed an army of 120,000 men, consisting of 80,000 Tatar cavalries and 40,000 Ottomans, which included 7,000 elite Janissaries. He led his army into Russian territory and headed toward Moscow.

By now, raids into Muscovy were nothing new. In fact, Rus lands had been habitually pillaged since the time of the Golden Horde. But what was novel was the scale of the invasion - Muscovy had 6,000 troops free to resist since the bulk of the army was engaged in a war with the Scandinavian kingdoms and Poland-Lithuania, and this number would normally have been enough. It also had a string of fortresses along the Oka River about 100 kilometers south of Moscow, built precisely to counter Tatar raids. However, Devlet I Giray completely bypassed the defenses, swinging deftly from the west toward Moscow.

Tatar and Ottoman light cavalry were consummate raiders. Their primary weapon was the composite bow, which they could fire with deadly accuracy on the move. Their lack of armor ensured a mobility that the heavy boyar cavalry could not match. The huge host depopulated villages and towns as it advanced, taking the young as slaves, massacring the old and weak, and burning their dwellings. The inadequate Muscovite force retreated to Moscow, where it stood a reasonable chance of repelling the enemy in a siege. Ottoman and Tatar raiders were not suited to siege warfare, though the contingent of Janissaries was. Approaching Moscow on May 24, the enemy pillaged the surrounding towns and suburbs, and a fire starting in the latter spread beyond the walls and into the city.

Muscovite citizens and the army struggled to contain the blaze, and within six hours, the whole city had completely burned down, and the commander of the army, Prince Belsky, was dead, having suffocated in his house. The death toll was horrific, and citizens rushing into the stone churches were crushed by collapsing stone. The powder magazine in the city fortress known as the Kremlin exploded, killing those who sought refuge there. Hundreds of Muscovites leaped into the Moscow River to escape the hellish firestorm, and many drowned. The palace was destroyed, though Tsar Ivan IV was not present. In fact, terrified of his possible reaction, his courtiers waited 10 days to tell him of the calamity.

Fires were not uncommon in Moscow, but the conflagration and invasion of 1571 was, by far, the greatest disaster Russia had suffered since the Mongol invasion of the 13th century. As many as 200,000 Muscovites may have perished,[10] and the Tsar had to forcibly remove people from other parts of Russia to repopulate the city. Beyond this catastrophe was the depopulation of the land between Crimea and Moscow and the 150,000 or so taken as captives to be sold in the markets of Caffa and Kherson.

Perhaps not surprisingly, the Crimean-Ottoman troops did not attempt to occupy Moscow after the inferno had passed. They were neither equipped nor suited for an occupation, and in any case, there was nothing left in the city to loot. They returned to Crimea through the smoking remains of villages and towns, devastating 36 more, including the city of Ryazan.

To counter the Ottomans, the Muscovite command had a plan. Prince Yuri Tokmakov sent a message from Moscow informing Vorotynsky that Tsar Ivan IV was marching from Novgorod with a huge army. This was a lie, but Tokmakov knew the messenger would be intercepted by the Tatars. Believing the intelligence, Khan Devlet I Giray felt compelled to resume the assault on August 2, the assault failed as had previous attacks, and the Muscovites broke their defenses to engage the enemy in close combat, rendering its bows useless. At the same time, Vorotynsky swept around the enemy host and attacked its rear while the Muscovite artillery, which could not fire behind the wooden walls, pounded the fleeing Tatars. By the end of the day, more than 25,000 Ottomans and Tatars had perished, including the sons and grandson of the Khan. Devlet I Giray barely escaped with his life and abandoned the standard of Islam on the battlefield. The Muscovites lost 6,000 at the most.

The defeat was more than a setback for the khanate. Though raids into Russia would continue regularly into the 18th century and the Crimean Tatars pillaged the suburbs of Moscow again in 1591 and 1592, the Tatars were no longer a threat to its very independence. Thus, the little-known Battle of Molodi was one of the most decisive battles in Russian and Tatar history.

---

[10] Travis, 2010, p. 171

As the Russian success indicated, European armies came to equal the Ottoman on the battlefield. The Ottoman military was still a potent force, but defeats became more frequent, and it became increasingly difficult to expand - let alone defend - imperial borders. Decreased expansion also meant a diminution of the elite sipahi cavalry, for with no fresh conquests, there were no new timars to be awarded.

The next direct conflict between Muscovy and the Ottoman Empire occurred in 1676 and was a consequence of the Polish-Ottoman War of 1672-76, during which the empire acquired the Ruthenian province of Podolia, now part of Ukraine, bordering the Ottoman vassal principality of Moldavia. It covered some 40,000 square kilometers, bordered by the Carpathian Mountains and the Dniester River in the west and extending eastward into the valley of the Southern Bug. The Bug gave access to the west bank of the Dnieper, and the towns of the Dnieper were within striking range of Ottoman troops.

The territory on both sides of the Dnieper - what is now Ukraine - was inhabited by the infamous Cossacks. The origin of the Cossacks is little understood, though they appear to have been the descendants of slaves who fled their masters. The Slav element predominated in Cossack society though there was a heavy Tatar influence as well. In 1660, the Cossacks split into two, each governed by a hetman (military governor), with those on the east bank of the Dnieper falling within the Muscovite sphere of influence and those to the west coming under Polish-Lithuanian tutelage. In 1669, Petro Doroshenko, hetman of the eastern Cossacks, successfully led a rebellion with Ottoman help and united the two groups. This outraged the Muscovites, for now the Ottomans could link up with both Doroshenko and the Crimean Tatars to strike at Moscow.

The Time of Troubles in Russia was well and truly over. After the wars with Poland-Lithuania, the medieval boyar army was gradually replaced by professional regiments, which included dragoons, *reiters* (light cavalry trained in the use of firearms), and the famous *Streltsy*, musketeers founded in the time of Ivan IV. The Muscovite Army also adopted the use of pike and borrowed hussars (heavy cavalry) from the Poles. These regiments formed about half of the Muscovite military in the latter half of the 17th century. The Russians, therefore, felt more confident in challenging the Ottomans than his predecessors.

Sergey Ivanov's painting of *Streltsy*

Meanwhile, the Ottoman military did not match the reforms of the European armies. This is not, however, to state that there were none at all during the 17th century, but they were relatively minor and concerned the manufacture and use of artillery and musketry. The Janissaries still resisted attempts at reform, as did the sipahi, who were not prepared to give up their timars to make way for a professional cavalry. Nevertheless, the Ottoman military remained one of the most efficient and experienced in Europe.

The Dawn of the 19th Century

In the summer of 1792, a German and French émigré army invaded France in an attempt to restore King Louis XVI, but on September 20 it was defeated by the revolutionary army. The following day, the French king was executed and France was declared a republic. Thereafter, Russia and the rest of Europe would be locked in a struggle with France that only ended after Napoleon was defeated at Waterloo in 1815. During that time, any plans for the conquest of the Ottoman Empire were put on hold.

Russian Empress Catherine the Great died of a stroke on November 17, 1796, and her son Paul, who certainly did not enjoy the confidence of his mother, became emperor. He reversed her expansionist policies and expressed no interest in conquering the Balkans before he was assassinated at the instigation of disgruntled nobles on March 24, 1801 and replaced by his eldest son, Alexander I. Alexander's efforts were directed against revolutionary France, and it was during his reign that Napoleon so disastrously invaded Russia in 1812.

Alexander I

Meanwhile, after the 1787–1792 war with Russia, Ottoman Sultan Selim III attempted to reform the Ottoman administration and military. Mindful that Russian artillery had been a decisive factor in Ottoman defeats, he created a new Artillery Corps with the help of French experts. He also created the *Nizam – I-Cedid*, the New Order Amy, modeled on European armies with modern weapons, organization, and training. It was intended to replace the conservative Janissary Corps, who consequently deposed him and replaced him with his mentally ill brother Mustafa IV in 1807.

The Russian war and the Janissary revolt weakened the Sultan's control over the Balkans, allowing Russia and Austria to encourage nationalist movements in the tumultuous provinces. The empire was further destabilized by Napoleon's invasion of Egypt in 1798, which aimed to damage British trade in the Middle East. The occupation drew not only the ire of the Ottomans but of the British, who defeated the French supporting fleet at the Battle of the Nile and thereafter maintained a keen interest in the fate of the Ottoman Empire. With interests in India and Persia, the British subsequently strove to ensure that no one power dominated the empire in general and Egypt in particular. This interest prolonged the life of the deteriorating Ottoman Empire, even as Britain was no less desirous of exploiting it than Russia or Austria.

The Eastern Question, which came to dominate the politics of Europe and the Near East in the 19th century, was no longer about how to push back an aggressive Ottoman Empire out of Europe but how to prevent it from collapsing and thereby strengthening a European rival. The "Sick Man of Europe"[11] was in danger of being despoiled by Russia and Austria, which were both suspicious of the other. Britain had a particular interest in ensuring that neither power dominated the Balkans, and the other great powers likewise nurtured interests in the Near East.

It was against this backdrop that the Ottoman Empire entered into its second period of decline. The first, which began after the Battle of Vienna in 1683, involved a still formidable power on the defensive for the first time in its history. After the Treaty of Jassy it was not only struggling to preserve its borders but its very existence. It fought to contain the Greek, Serbian, Bulgarian and Romanian nationalist movements, encouraged by Russia and inspired by the French Revolution. Russia, reaching out to Persia and Armenia, destabilized the Ottoman Empire's eastern borders as well, and in Egypt, Britain and France supported the separatist movement in Islamic Egypt.

This is not to suggest that the Ottoman Empire was utterly incapable of reforming itself and resisting. Sultan Mahmud II, who assumed the throne in 1808, succeeded in dissolving the Janissaries and restoring Selim III's New Order Army, and he subsequently embarked on a series of Westernizing reforms. Ultimately, however, the reforms came too late, and the Ottoman military remained years behind the Western Europeans.

---

[11] Harold Temperley, *England and the Near East* (London: Longmans, Greens and Co., 1936), p. 272.

Mahmud II

Throughout the 19th century, Russia still fondly nurtured the dream of controlling the Balkans and Constantinople, but it would be the Europeans, not the Ottomans, would prevent it. In 1806, Sultan Selim III's government was torn between Napoleon's French Empire and Russia - the invasion of Egypt had compelled it to accept a defensive alliance with Russia and Britain, but under the influence of French Ambassador Horace Sebastiani, and emboldened by Napoleon's victory over the Russians and Austrians at Austerlitz in December 1805, Selim III decided to throw in his lot with the French. He was dealing with a rebellion in Serbia, begun in 1804 and supported by Russia, and he hoped Napoleon would give assistance from his bases in Dalmatia, newly acquired from Austria.

With that in mind, the Ottoman government closed the Dardanelles to Russian shipping and deposed the Russophile vassal princes of Moldavia and Wallachia. This prompted Russian Emperor Alexander I to step up aid to the Serbs and begin preparing for war. For a time, Selim, under intense pressure from the British and an anti-war party at home, vacillated, reinstating the deposed princes and agreeing to re-open the Dardanelles. He was facing a revolt of the

Janissaries at the time that threatened to escalate into a civil war.

The revolt was a reaction to the creation of the Nizam-i Djedit, the New Order Army, based on a Western organisation, Western technology, and French training, which Selim considered vital to fighting a war in the 19th century. He attempted to introduce it surreptitiously, but it rapidly drew the ire of not only the Janissaries but also elements of the population opposed to foreign influence, conscription, and higher taxes imposed to pay for the military reforms. New Order troops clashed with the Janissaries, and Selim only avoided a full-scale war by withdrawing his army to Constantinople in September 1806 and forming a new government with both reformist and conservative ministers. Under these circumstances, war with Russia was unthinkable.

On October 14, 1806, Napoleon dealt a crushing blow to the Prussians, and Berlin was occupied 13 days later. Russia was now deprived of continental allies against the French Empire, and a pact with France seemed more attractive. Selim removed the Moldavian and Wallachian governors for the second time and refused to open the Dardanelles to Russia. At the same time, the Ottomans began preparations for war, which worried Emperor Alexander, who moved troops to northern Europe to prepare for a confrontation with the French. The Russian emperor urged the British to apply pressure to keep the Ottomans neutral and open the Dardanelles, but Selim declared war on Russia on December 24. Russia invaded Moldavia and Wallachia, meeting little resistance, and a British squadron under Sir John Duckworth engaged the Ottoman Navy and coastal forts in an unsuccessful attempt to force open the Dardanelles. The British occupation of Alexandria in Egypt in February was more successful, though attempts to progress further were thwarted at the Battle of Rosetta in March.

Perhaps emboldened by the popularity generated by the defense of Constantinople and the Dardanelles, Selim III once more attempted to reform the military. He sent one of his ministers to persuade the Bosporus troops to adopt New Order uniforms, but they protested and murdered him on May 25. The troops then marched about 20 miles to Constantinople under elected leader Kabakçı Mustafa, and the commander of the nearby New Order contingent refused to move against him. Two days later, Kabakçı Mustafa was in Constantinople, Selim III was deposed, and the reformist leaders were earmarked for execution. Selim's cousin was installed as Mustafa IV, while the Janissaries went on a murderous rampage through the capital.

Unbeknownst to the Ottoman government at this time, Napoleon was no longer interested in an alliance, and the Ottoman ambassador to Paris was ignored. In fact, the French emperor contemplated peace with Prussia and Russia and saw Alexander as a potential ally. On July 7, 1807, 16 days after an Ottoman counteroffensive was halted at the Battle of Obilesti, Alexander I and Napoleon signed a treaty at Tilsit in East Prussia. Russia was to leave Moldavia and Wallachia to work for peace with the Ottomans. In secret dealings, France and Russia agreed to partition the Ottoman Empire if the peace failed, with Russia obtaining the lion's share. In return, Russia would join in the European blockade of Britain.

Worrying for the new regime in Constantinople was the Ottoman Army on the Danube under the command of Alemdar Mustafa Pasha, a reformist supporter of Selim III. The armistice preceding the Peace of Tilsit allowed him to march on Constantinople to restore the deposed sultan. On June 21, he entered Constantinople unopposed with 15,000 men and ordered the arrest of the rebels, who were executed or exiled. In a frantic endeavour to save his life, Mustafa IV commanded the deaths of the two remaining males of the House of Osman, presuming that Alemdar would have no choice but to confirm him as sultan. Selim III was strangled, but Mustafa's younger brother, Mahmud, was saved by the intervention of Alemdar's men. Mustafa was deposed (later executed) and the 23-year-old prince became Mahmud II on July 28, 1808. Alemdar Mustafa Pasha became grand vizier and the reformist party seized power, though an attempt to revive the New Order Army failed later in that year. Nevertheless, reform would come, and Mahmud would be the Sultan to accomplish it.

With the armistice between Russia and the Ottoman Empire coming to an end, Alexander transferred troops from northern Europe in preparation for a Balkans offensive in 1809. In January of that year, Britain, now at war with both France and its new ally, Russia, made peace with Constantinople. Britain guaranteed the integrity of the Ottoman Empire, ensuring that no foreign warships should enter the Dardanelle Straits. It further pledged to use its fleet to protect Constantinople in return for commercial privileges.

In August, Prince Peter Bagration took over the Russian command and laid siege to Silistria on the southern bank of the Danube (Bulgaria). The town was important to the Ottomans on account of its command of transport with and communication to the Black Sea. However, as soon as he learned of the approach of a 50,000-strong relief army, he withdrew to Moldavia beyond the Prut River.

Russia renewed the offensive in the spring of 1810 without Bagration, who had been called away for a war with Sweden, and this time, Silistria fell on May 30, though the city of Shumen (about 100 miles to the south) repelled the invaders. On August 26 at Batin, an army of 20,000 Russians routed an Ottoman army twice its size, thus gaining possession of the Danube Delta.

Important as the Russians' victories were, Constantinople was still not in any immediate danger, and Russia's relations with Napoleon, always strained, had reached a breaking point. The French had not sent assistance in the Balkan war as they had promised. Moreover, the continental blockade was hurting Russia, and Alexander found ways to continue trading with Britain. He also objected to the creation of the Grand Duchy of Poland, which he felt could be used for an invasion of Russia. Accordingly, he directed his generals to bring the war to a decisive conclusion.

The emperor was taken aback when, after soundly defeating the Ottomans under Grand Vizier Ahmed Pasha at Ruse in northern Bulgaria on June 22, 1811, General Michael Kutuzov withdrew his force of about 450,000 toward the Prut. The Ottomans, thinking they had somehow won a victory, crossed the Danube in pursuit, whereupon Kutuzov turned around, cut off Ahmed's supplies and line of retreat, and routed the Ottomans on October 2. Ahmed lost 9,000 men out of an army of 70,000, and the survivors were encircled without food and supplies. Rather than starve them into submission, Kutuzov sent them provisions, a move he justified to the emperor by arguing that saving large numbers of hostages would give Russia more leverage at the negotiating table.

Kutuzov was right, as Ahmed Pasha surrendered on November 23 and Mahmud signified his willingness to negotiate. The Treaty of Bucharest was signed on May 28, 1812, the same time as Napoleon prepared his Grande Armée to invade Russia. Mahmud knew that despite the disastrous performance of his armies, he could press for the least onerous terms. Russia obtained only Moldavia between the Prut and Dniester (Bessarabia) and trading rights in the Danube. Serbia received a measure of autonomy, and in Transcaucasia, where there had been fighting since 1807, there were few territorial changes. The Ottoman government survived, not by the might of arms but by diplomacy and happenstance. While Russia and Austria fought Napoleon, it was secure, though it desperately needed to reform.

Through it all, Ottoman society was deeply divided over Westernization. The sultan's party saw it as a necessity, while the religious establishment and most of the populace viewed it as a betrayal of Islam. On top of that, the next conflict with Russia would once again highlight that no matter how much Westernization was attempted, the inadequacies of the Ottoman government and military remained, and tensions between reformists and conservatives would turn to violence.

The Greek Revolution and the War of 1829-30

In 1815, Napoleon was defeated at Waterloo and a peace, of sorts, returned to Europe. The Congress of Vienna redrew the map of Europe, with Russia, Austria, Prussia, and Great Britain presiding over it. The final settlement, drawn up by the statesmen of Vienna, made no declaration concerning the Ottoman Empire, nor was the Sultan invited to send a representative. The empire's integrity was considered a question for Russia, Austria, and Great Britain, and none of them wanted it decided by a European congress. After the Congress of Vienna, Austria's Emperor Alexander organised a league of states called the Holy Alliance, which consisted of Russia, Austria, and Prussia and was an ostensibly Christian association intended to exclude the Islamic Ottoman Empire. Thus, the small window by which the Ottoman state might have taken a place in the concert of Europe was closed.

Though isolated, the Ottoman Empire would certainly not be ignored, and a crisis in the Balkans would inevitably attract the great powers' attention. Such a crisis unfolded in 1821 when the Ottoman Empire's Greek subjects revolted to make war upon the Sultan's troops.

Throughout the 19th century and the beginning of the 20th century, the rise of nationalistic aspirations largely contributed to the decline of the Ottoman Empire. The concept of "nation" was new to the Ottoman Empire, which had thus far thought of his subjects as communities built on religion rather than language or geographic origins. To deal with the challenges resulting from the existence of several religions within the empire, the system of millet was created after Sultan Mehmed II conquered Constantinople. This system guaranteed that Christians, and later other religions, would be able to live under Ottoman law by allowing them to choose their own religious leaders, collect their taxes, use their own language and have their own court. While equality between the different subjects of the empire was not achieved (nor was it an actual goal until the Tanzimat era), the system made it possible for communities to live side by side. This system also preserved or created singularities among the various peoples of the empire. In a sense, while the Millet system did indeed help the empire's expansion and social stability for a time, it also prevented the tackling the issue of its identity, until it was too late, while also preserving, strengthening and helping to create new identities.

One of the strongest identities maintained through the Orthodox Church was a powerful elite group known as the *Phanariotes*, a Greek one. The existing Greek nationalistic sentiment had already been stirred by Russia, which saw the Greeks as allies in the struggle against the Ottomans. The new Russian intelligentsia saw the emerging Empire as the successor of the Byzantine Empire. This heritage was underlined by Russia's coat of arms, the double-headed eagle, formerly associated with Constantinople and the Eastern Roman Empire. On the political level, this narrative was seen as a way to influence the various peoples under Ottoman rule in the Balkans by attracting those who sought independence. It was no coincidence that Alexander Ypsilantis, a central figure of the Greek independence movement, served in the Russian army. However, the context of the uprising that broke out in 1821 made it different from previous revolts sponsored by Russia.

Ypsilantis

The aspirations of the peoples ruled by the Ottomans were fueled by the ideas of the French Revolution in 1789. The revolution saw the emergence of the concept of "patrie" (Fatherland) and pitted the "patriotes" against the old nobility. The Greeks were particularly influenced by new ideas coming from Western Europe. Greek merchants travelled through Europe while elements among the Greek elite, the Phanariotes, cultivated their difference and supported the diffusion of such ideas by financing schools and books promoting it. This growth of the Greek national culture and sentiment, known as the Modern Greek Enlightenment, resulted in the sentiment among Greeks that they were part of one separate nation. In 1814, in the Russian city of Odessa,[12] these ideas led to the creation of a new secret society, the *Filiki Eteria* or Society of Friends, aimed at ending the Ottoman rule over Greece. The society attracted many members of the Greek diaspora. This included Ypsilantis, who became the head of the society on July 15, 1820, after the then Russian Foreign Minister and Ionian-born Ioannis Antonios Kapodistrias refused it.

Ypsilantis and the leaders of the *Filiki Eteria* designed a plan to obtain Greece's independence. At this time, while the Greek national sentiment was growing, the borders of the new country were uncertain, with some members of the society even backing the revival of the Byzantine

---

[12] Present day Ukraine.

Empire. Ypsilantis himself saw his fight as a broader struggle that should involve all the Christian subjects of the Empire, both for ideological and strategic purposes. He, along with other members of the secret society, felt that previous revolts in the region failed due to the lack of coordination between the organizers of the revolts. He thus drafted a plan that would involve simultaneous revolts led by Greeks, Serbs, Montenegrins, as well the subjects of Wallachia (present day Romania), Bulgaria and Moldavia.

In February 1821, with a small force of troops, Ypsilantis crossed the Prut River into Ottoman-held Moldavia, defeating the Turks and calling for a revolt in the Peloponnese and among Christian subjects of the Empire. Claiming he had secured the support of Russia, Ypsilantis was backed by Tudor Vladimirescu, the leader of the Wallachian Pandur militia, who occupied Bucharest on March 21. In Greece, Theodoros Kolokotronis, a member of the *Filiki Eteria,* captured the city of Tripolitsa in the Peloponnese, spreading the revolt to central Greece, Crete and Macedonia. Within a year, the revolutionaries took control of the Peloponnese and later repelled several Ottoman invasions.

Despite this success, the revolution was threatened both from within and from without. Ypsilantis's revolt in the Danube region had turned into a crushing defeat as Russia disavowed his campaign. The Tsar was then part of the Holy Alliance signed after the defeat of Napoleon that sought to preserve the status quo in Europe and prevent the circulation of revolutionary ideas. As a result, Vladimirescu withdrew his support for Ypsilantis as Ottoman troops crossed the Danube River and forced his retreat. In Greece, rivalries and dissensions between several factions within the liberated territories as well as between inhabitants of the Peloponnese and of central Greece hindered the war effort, eventually leading to a civil war.

The Greeks also faced an initially limited Egyptian intervention in Crete and Cyprus. The success of the Egyptian contingent eventually convinced the Ottomans to call for a broader intervention by Muhammad Ali Pasha, the Wali of Egypt, despite their defiance for the ambitious governor. During the years that followed, spearheaded by Egyptian troops, the Ottomans almost fully reconquered Greece, taking Athens in 1826.

Ultimately, the revolution was only saved by the intervention of European powers. While initially the *Holy Alliance* and its principles had prevented any intervention from European powers, public opinion shifted in favor of the insurgents quickly. The hanging of the Orthodox Patriarch Gregory V on suspicion of colluding with the rebels shocked the Europeans, and the support of inspiring figures such as Lord Byron, who fought alongside the rebels, helped grow the revolutionaries' support among the European nations. Britain, France and Russia signed the Treaty of London in 1827, calling for a cessation of hostilities, and stipulating that in case the Sultan would refuse, the powers could act to enforce such a cessation of hostilities. After the Sultan refused, Britain, France and Russia sent their fleets to the Peloponnese to pressure the Sultan. While it was initially only meant to prevent the Ottoman fleet from reaching the island of

Hydra, an initial incident between a British boat and an Egyptian one triggered broader confrontations, resulting in the destruction of the Ottoman fleet during the Battle of Navarino. France later sent an expeditionary corps and, alongside the reorganized Greek forces, defeated the Ottomans at the Battle of Petra, in central Greece, leading eventually to the full independence of Greece in 1832.

A depiction of the patriarch shortly before his execution

Lord Byron

The revolution wasn't the first successful revolt against the Ottomans, but it was certainly a game-changer. For the first time, the Ottoman Empire was forced to recognize the full independence of a nation, not because of a war with a foreign power or an ambitious governor, but because of the aspirations of its people. The Filiki Eteria's attempt to prompt a larger uprising among Christians in the Balkans, despite being thwarted by the prompt Ottoman offensive, also left its mark in the memories of the Empire's subjects.

Moreover, the growing mistrust between the Empire and its subjects continued to be used by foreign powers such as Russia to weaken the Empire. The cause of the Ottoman Christians continued to be extremely popular among Europeans. As further shown by the initial intervention of the European powers, however, the goal was almost never to directly confront the Ottoman Empire, at least for England and France.

After the Greeks succeeded, it had to seem to the rest of the empire that its subjugated peoples could rise against their rulers, and Mahmud no doubt suspected that more was to come. Along with the unrest among Christians, he also saw displeasure arise in the capital and among the upper classes. He had inherited an empire in a dire economical condition, and the uprisings and wars had not helped the treasury. His reforms had mostly helped alleviate the financial burden of the lower classes and even out some of the extreme differences between the rich and poor, and in his own government he got rid of both titles and employees with no real function, but there was more to accomplish. Mahmud streamlined efficiency and organized the imperial household so as to control the excessive spending within the court. He even implemented changes in the provincial administrations to find corruption and again clean up among the old offices. He also founded institutions to train new government personnel and founded the first newspaper in the Ottoman-Turkish language, a required read for all his citizens.

The most notorious act he is remembered for is what would come to be known as The Auspicious Incident. In 1826, he abolished the Janissaries. Though the Janissaries had enjoyed a certain level of authority and managed to depose and install a number of sultans in the past centuries, they had become an unruly force to the sultans and the people. The first decades of the 19th century had seen an increased resistance and in some cases outright hatred for the elite corps as they misused their privileges and oppressed civilians. The army had needed a reorganization for many years when Mahmud came to power, but the conducted reforms had always been fought back and suppressed by the Janissaries. Now, Mahmud spread the rumor that he was forming another elite corps, Sekban-i Cedit, and when the Janissaries revolted on the streets of Constantinople as Mahmud anticipated, he deployed the Sipahis, the cavalry, to fight them back. Alongside them, ordinary citizens were also eager to chase the Janissaries away.

This uprising was the final straw, and by defeating them in their treacherous act, Mahmud could formally disband the Janissaries and have most of them executed on the spot, eagerly supported by the citizens and the army. This all took place as the fighting in Greece was still ongoing, and Mahmud had to push his military reforms into being while at war with the powerful alliance of Russia, France, and Britain.

Meanwhile, in response to Mahmud's denial of Greek autonomy and the imminent collapse of the uprising, the three signatories of the Treaty of London assembled a fleet consisting of three squadrons. The British squadron of 12 ships was the largest, with the Russians having eight and the French seven. In total, the allies commanded 10 ships of the line and 10 frigates. It was under the overall command of Sir Edward Codrington, a veteran of the Battle of Trafalgar. He was under orders to impede Ottoman reinforcements to Greece and to impose an armistice but not to engage the Ottomans unless compelled to do so.

The Ottoman fleet of 88 ships was far superior in terms of numbers, though it possessed only three ships of the line. It was commanded by Ibrahim Pasha, who initially promised Codrington that he would negotiate with the Greeks, but the Egyptian admiral was outraged that Codrington did not prevent rebel activity and moreover, had attacked Ottoman positions.

In fact, Codrington's men had acted on their own initiatives, ignoring their admiral's instructions. Ibrahim Pasha resumed hostilities, and Codrington took the fateful step of facing off against the Ottoman fleet in the Bay of Navarino (modern Pylos) on the western coast of Messenia in the Peloponnese on October 20, 1827. Ibrahim Pasha demanded they withdraw, and Codrington refused.

The allies claimed the Ottomans had been the first to open fire, but regardless of who began the firing, by the end of the day, the Ottoman fleet was destroyed, with the loss of 80 vessels and about 3,000 dead, while the allies lost not a single ship.

Mahmud II had no choice but to close the Dardanelles, lest the Russian Black Sea Fleet attack Constantinople. This was bound to provoke the Russians, who were still not technically at war. He also repudiated a convention made in 1826 by which Moldavia and Wallachia elected their own princes, who were then appointed by Constantinople. Russia declared war and moved into the Romanian principalities with 100,000 men, personally commanded by Nicholas I. By June 1828, they had crossed the Danube, and on September 29, they laid siege to Varna with the support of the Black Sea Fleet under Alexsey Greig. At Shumai, however, the 40,000-strong Ottoman garrison repelled an army suffering from disease and shortages, and by the winter, the invasion force had withdrawn back to Bessarabia, leaving a besieging force at Varna.

In February 1829, Nicholas returned to St. Petersburg, leaving command to the German-born Field Marshal Hans Karl Von Diebitsch, who resumed the offensive in the spring. On June 11, an army of 40,000 Ottomans sent to relieve Varna was soundly defeated, after which Diebitsch headed south with 35,000 men. On August 22, he entered Adrianople (Edirne), an imperial city about 200 miles west of Constantinople. No Russian army had ever been so close to the Ottoman capital.

On the Caucasian Front, the Russians advanced steadily as far as Erzurum in northeast Anatolia. Russian troops in the region had just made peace with Persia (February 1828) and thus were battle-ready. The purpose of the eastern offensive was not so much to capture territory but to tie down Ottoman troops and prevent sea-landings on the Black Sea coast.

With Constantinople within striking distance and Russian troops encroaching into Anatolia, the Ottomans sued for peace. The Treaty of Adrianople was signed on September 14, 1829 and made extensive concessions to the Russian Empire. The Ottomans had to pay a war indemnity, and Wallachia and Moldavia were occupied as sureties. Russia acquired fortresses in Georgia and right of access to the Danube Delta. All Russian merchants within the Ottoman Empire were considered under the protection of the Russian ambassador to Constantinople, and the Dardanelles were to be opened to commercial vessels As for Greece, it was to be granted autonomy according to the terms of the Treaty of London.

However, the terms of Adrianople were not satisfactory to Britain and France, who felt it conceded too much influence to Russia. The two powers conceived the idea - rejected until then - of an independent Greece as a means of countering Russian influence. Nicholas I reluctantly agreed, and they decided that the new nation should be a monarchy. They selected Otto von Wittelsbach, the second son of King Ludwig I of Bavaria, to be its first king. Otto chose to rule as an absolute monarch, much to the satisfaction of Emperor Nicholas, but not so much to that of the Greeks, who had shed their blood for liberal democracy.

The great powers had intervened in the Greek crisis with the intention of preserving the stability of the Ottoman Empire. Russia, Britain, and France favored autonomy, and this would have been achieved by the Russian victory in 1829 had the British and French, anxious about Russia's power in the Balkans, not pressed for independence. As it happened, an independent Greece destabilized the Ottoman state even further. The nascent state consisted of the Peloponnese, Attica (the region around Athens), central Greece, and some of the Aegean Islands - less than half of present-day Greece - but Greek populations were scattered throughout southern Rumelia, Anatolia, and the Eastern Mediterranean. A number of islands, including Crete and Cyprus, remained under Ottoman control. The Greeks were not content to be contained in a peninsula but aspired to a *Megali Hellas* ("Great Greece") that would encompass all the lands inhabited by Greeks during the time of the Byzantine Empire, including Constantinople.[13] The idea would dominate Greek foreign policy until the 1920s.

The war over Greece had humiliated the Ottomans once again, and the empire found itself isolated and without friends. One positive change emerged, however, and that was the quelling of the revolt of the Janissaries and their consequent and perpetual extinction. The path to much-needed and overdue reform had been opened, and Mahmud II embarked upon it with determination and gusto. He reformed the military and abolished the feudal system by which land was granted in return for military service. He ordered the remodelling of the navy and the artillery corps. He adopted Western models of government and reformed the traditional bureaucracy. He wore Western-style clothing but mandated the wearing of the fez as a distinguishing feature.

After Mahmud died in 1839, his son, Abdulmejid I, continued these reforms, instituting a new model of government named Ottomanism. This re-established the Ottoman state on the basis of common citizenship regardless of religion and ethnicity. All inhabitants of the empire possessed (in theory) equal rights under the law, including freedom of religion. Ottomanization was intended as a counter to Western-inspired nationalism and was a bold idea, but in the end, it

---

[13] Daskalov and Marinov, 2013, p. 200

satisfied neither the liberals nor the conservative Islamic faction and contributed to the further destabilization of the empire.

The Crimean War

The next conflict between the Ottoman Empire and Russia was not the result of aggression on either's part but occurred at a time when, paradoxically, the two empires were technically allies for the first time in history. Though it is known as the Crimean War, the peninsula was not the subject of dispute.

In 1830, France occupied Ottoman Algeria, and in the same year, Mahmud II recognized Serbia as an autonomous principality. The following year saw Viceroy of Egypt Muhammad Ali claim independence and invade Syria with the ultimate intention of deposing Mahmud II. His successes worried the Ottoman government, which agreed to an alliance with Russia in return for a guarantee that the Dardanelles would be closed to any European power's warships at Russia's request. Nicholas I then dispatched an army (which may have been as large as 40,000 men[14]) to block Muhammad Ali's path to Constantinople.

The move had the desired effect as the Egyptians negotiated a truce, but the British were not comfortable with Russian troops so close to Constantinople, and a treaty had potentially given the Russian navy the sole right to navigate the Dardanelle Straits. The London Straits Convention of 1841 established that the Straits were demilitarized except for Ottoman warships and those of its allies in times of war, but tensions between the great powers remained.

It was France that set a chain of events in motion that led to war in 1853. Louis Napoleon Bonaparte, the nephew of the famous Napoleon, had transformed the Second French Republic into the Second Empire with himself in power as Emperor Napoleon III. He was anxious to rehabilitate France's reputation, marred by three revolutions between 1789 and 1848 and the Napoleonic Wars, and win back prestige. He needed to gain the support of the Catholic Church and wished to project himself as its champion at home and abroad. Already, he had guaranteed Rome and the Papal States against the movement for Italian unification, and now he claimed "sovereign authority" over Catholic Christians in the Ottoman Empire, particularly in Palestine.[15]

Emperor Nicholas I was furious, for Russia claimed the right of protection over Orthodox Christians in the Ottoman state and could not tolerate Catholics being given equal or even superior status. He induced Abdulmejid I to confirm Russia's rights, whereupon, in 1853, Napoleon III ordered a 90-gun steamship, named after Charlemagne, another forceful emperor, to sail through the Dardanelles in clear violation of the Straits Convention, the effect of which was a declaration from the Ottomans that Catholics would have authority over the Orthodox on

---

[14] Kinross, 1977, p. 468

[15] Trevor, 2000

sacred Christian sites in Palestine.

Russia responded by mobilizing troops on the Danube (it still occupied Wallachia and Moldavia since the Ottomans had not yet paid the indemnity imposed from the previous war) and placing diplomatic pressure on the Ottoman government. On May 31, 1853, Russian Ambassador Menshikov delivered an ultimatum for a protectorate over Orthodox Christians, but when it was rejected - with British support - Nicholas did not declare war; he still hoped to avoid armed conflict with Britain and France and protested he had no territorial demands on the Ottoman government. He was worried about Austria, too. He had supposed it would allow Russian troops to invade Rumelia out of gratitude for the Russians having helped suppress a nationalist revolt in Hungary in 1848, but in truth, the government of Emperor Franz Josef I was deeply suspicious and would not rule out going to war.

The British and French responded to the ultimatum by sending warships to the Dardanelles (June 8), whereupon the Russians moved troops into Moldavia (July 2). As of yet, no parties had sought out a military confrontation, but as diplomacy continued to fail, Abdulmejid I, conscious that the Ottoman Empire was in the more powerful position and confident that France and Britain would support him, broke off diplomatic relations and declared war on October 5. By the end of the month, Ottoman troops had crossed the Romanian border, and British warships - still technically neutral - were in the Bosporus.

The first pitched battle occurred on November 4, when an Ottoman force of 8,000 under Omar Pasha occupied the Danubian port of Oltenita as part of a campaign to take Bucharest. General Peter Dannenberg moved against them with 6,000 men. Omar Pasha repelled him, albeit with heavy losses. The Russians put their failure down to a lack of heavy artillery, and while this was undoubtedly true, the army that bested them was not the same army they had fought in the Greek War. In the period following the extirpation of the Janissaries, Mahmud II and Abdulmejid I had made military reform a priority. The armies that had met the Russians in 1853 were modeled and organised along Western lines with a general staff and well-defined chain of command. There were six armies, totaling about 664,000 men, though levies could also be called up. They were not of the same caliber as the British and French, but the war would highlight serious shortcomings in all the belligerent armies, especially concerning the quality of command and supply issues.

On November 30, a squadron of 12 Ottoman warships including two steamers was destroyed by a force of 11 Russian vessels at Sinop on the Black Sea coast, mid-way between Constantinople and the eastern border, and in January 1854, the French and British fleets entered the Black Sea as a wave of popular sentiment for the Ottomans swept their nations. As Britain and France were still not the Sultan's allies, they were in violation of the Straits Convention.

Two days after Sinop, the Ottomans defeated the Russians in Romania at the Battle of Citate, but further to the south, King Otto of Greece decided to take advantage of the conflict to occupy

Thessaly, further exacerbating France and Britain's anxieties. On February 10, a British delegation met with Nicholas I but failed to secure a peace. Finally, on February 27, Britain and France delivered an ultimatum to withdraw from Wallachia and Moldavia. Austria supported the demand and did not guarantee its neutrality in the event of war. The Kingdom of Prussia also expressed its anxiety about the Russian presence in the Balkans. Russia's response was to cross the Danube, and lay siege to Silistria in Bulgaria, whereupon France and Britain declared war on March 28.

On April 18, the Ottoman Army defeated the Russians again at Rohova on the Romanian-Bulgarian border, while British and French troops occupied the Greek port of Piraeus to prevent the Greeks sending help to Russia. They also bombarded the Black Sea port of Odessa. Meanwhile, Austria sent large numbers of troops into Wallachia and Moldavia with the consent of the Ottoman government, clearly warning the Russians to withdraw. By the end of May, there were some 50,000 soldiers from the Imperial Austrian Army on the move, prompting the Russians to lift the siege of Silistria on June 9. Around this time, a British-French expeditionary force landed at Varna to assist the Ottomans. By the end of July, the Russians had crossed the Pruth and withdrawn to Bessarabia. On the Caucasian Front, the Russians fared better, soundly defeating an Ottoman army at Kurekdere (Gyumri, Armenia) on August 6, though without progress in the Balkans, the victory had little effect. In the Black Sea, the Russian fleet remained at the port in Sevastopol without daring to engage the British, who were the undoubted masters of naval warfare.

Russian armies had left the Balkan provinces, Constantinople was secure, and the empire enjoyed the protection of Austria, Britain, France, and Prussia. It remained only to propose a peace settlement, but Abdulmejid's goals differed widely from those of France and Britain. The Ottoman government talked of strengthening its presence in Moldavia and Wallachia so as to make the future protection of the great powers unnecessary, and the suzerainty over the Crimea, Georgia, and Circassia was restored.[16] France had broader geopolitical goals which would increase France's prestige and power in Europe, whereas the British were intent on ending the Russian naval threat to Constantinople and thence to the eastern Mediterranean. Moreover, public opinion, which did not appreciate that victory had been gained by diplomacy, naval superiority, and the blood of the Ottomans demanded more tangible proof. Therefore, the three powers proposed a peace on terms the Russians were almost certain to reject: the renunciation of protectorates over Wallachia and Moldavia, abandoning claims over Orthodox Christians, a revision of the 1841 Straits Convention, and freedom of trade for all nations along the Danube. The Russians predictably rejected these conditions, and the war continued.

The Austrian intervention had effectively neutralised the Balkans as a theatre though minor actions continued until the end of the war, and so the allies determined that Sevastopol on the Crimean Peninsula should become their objective. Sevastopol was the principal base of the

---

[16] Baumgart, 2020, p. 36

Russian Black Sea Fleet and was thus, in theory, a logical choice, but the campaign was poorly planned and executed. The allies landed fairly easily in September 1854 but failed to take advantage of their victory at Alma (September 20). Had they pursued the enemy, Sevastopol probably would have fallen. As it happened, the bloody siege of Sevastopol lasted almost a year.

From this point, the war became the Crimean War and was, from the point of view of the English-speaking public and popular historians, a British war. In point of fact, the largest allied contingent during the Siege of Sevastopol was French with 75,000 men, followed by Ottomans and Egyptians with 72,000. In fact, the British never had more than 35,000 present,[17] and though operations could not have been possible without their naval presence, the land campaign could not have succeeded without the French and the Ottomans. Piedmont also sent 15,000, and 15,500 foreign volunteers arrived from Germany, Switzerland, Poland, and Italy[18] to face over 100,000 Russians.

Ottoman troops were present at most of the great battles of the Sevastopol campaign: Balaclava (October 26, 1854), Eupatoria (February 17, 1855), and Charnaya (August 16, 1855). At Eupatoria, they formed the largest allied contingent - 30,000 - with three French cavalry regiments, and naval support repelled a similar number of Russians. Here and in other battles, the newly reformed Ottoman Army acquitted itself well, yet the Anglo-French command refused to use it to the best advantage. This was largely due to prejudice, but also, the French and British did not want the Ottomans to attain a prestige that would allow them to speak against their interests at a negotiating table.

As the Siege of Sevastopol continued, the Russians increased the intensity of their offensive in the Caucasus to shift troops to the eastern theatre. General Michael Muraviev was given 40,000 men and instructed to take the Armenian city of Kars, which commanded a route into the Turkish heartland. The morale of the 17,000-strong garrison was low until Lord Raglan, commander-in-chief of the allied force, sent General William Fenwick Williams to take charge toward the end of 1854. In the spring of the following year, the renewed garrison repelled two assaults, prompting Muraviev to opt for a conventional siege.

In the Crimea, Omar Pasha, the Ottoman field marshal, successfully persuaded Raglan to allow him to go to Armenia with 45 000, but instead of relieving Kars, he marched on to engage the Russians in Georgia. He left Kars to his son, Selim Pasha, who arrived at Trebizond (Trabzon) with 15,000 men in September, but even these did not reach Kars, and the exhausted garrison surrendered on November 28.

On August 28, 1855, the fortress of Sevastopol finally fell after an intense bombardment and assault and after the Russians had abandoned the city, but the victory left the allies in something

---

[17] Maule, *1908/2009*
[18] Chandler, 1980, p.146

of a quandary. The objective had been obtained, yet it remained doubtful as to how the Russians could be made to sue for peace. After all, the allied campaign had been manageable - infamous failures of leadership, communication, and logistics aside - but conquering the rest of the peninsula, let alone contemplating an invasion of Ukraine, presented almost insurmountable challenges. Moreover, reports of excessive casualties, operational blunders, and death from poor hygiene - despite Florence Nightingale's best efforts - were generating public opposition to the war.

Emperor Nicholas I was resolute against peace, but he had died on March 5, 1855, and his successor, Alexander II, was more amenable to peace talks. He was not a liberal, but at the same time, he was not as reactionary as Nicholas. He also realized that Russia had ultimately lost the war because it had failed to match the reforms - technological, industrial, military, economic, and social - of Western Europe. The catalyst for peace was Austria, which threatened to enter the war on the allied side, and on February 1, 1856, he agreed to negotiate. At the Congress of Paris, the great powers - Austria, Britain, France, Prussia, and Russia - guaranteed the integrity of the Ottoman Empire. Russia renounced its claim of the protection of Christians in Ottoman territory and restored all territory seized in the Balkans and in Armenia. Sevastopol was returned to Russia, but the Black Sea was declared a demilitarised zone, meaning that no warships, including Ottoman, could navigate it. The Danube was pronounced free to the merchant vessels of all powers.

The human cost of the Crimean War was colossal, and the conflict is often counted as the first modern war in terms of its carnage and impact on entire nations. Most soldiers died not in battle but of disease. The Ottoman Empire lost over 45,000 men,[19] almost a quarter of the total allied casualties, in contrast with 530,000 Russian dead. The Ottomans mobilized a total of 165,000 troops and lost over a third. Russia mobilised 889,000 and lost more than half that number. In strategic and diplomatic terms, the undoubted loser was the Russian Empire. Its exclusion from the Black Sea and the Balkans constituted a devastating humiliation and set back its ambitions in those regions by decades. It had effectively been relegated to the status of a second-rate power. The defeat highlighted the backwardness of Russian society, which was still essentially medieval, with most of the population in legal serfdom. Alexander II would liberate the serfs (with little real benefit to the peasantry) and institute other reforms. Nevertheless, reform never went far enough, and tensions between the autocrat regime and the reform movement would stifle meaningful change until the empire collapsed in 1917.

The Ottoman Empire benefitted from the peace in that the powers guaranteed its integrity. It was also granted a seat at the diplomatic congresses of Europe for the first time and could make representations concerning its own future. On the other hand, it was certainly not on a par with the great powers, all of which still considered it the "Sick Man of Europe," the preservation of which was a burden necessary to prevent a European war. Abdulmejid wanted his state to stand

---

[19] Clodfelter, 2017, p. 180

as an equal, but the Ottomans found themselves dependent on the Royal Navy and Austria, in particular. The peace did not even permit the Ottomans a free hand in their own dominions: Moldavia and Wallachia were to be granted self-rule, Serbia was to be unhindered as it strove toward full independence, and Bulgaria agitated for freedom. Egypt was practically an independent state and under the watchful eyes of Great Britain, and Russia almost immediately began diplomatic efforts to address its humiliation and to seek revenge on the Ottomans.

Furthermore, the dependence upon the great powers, particularly Britain and France, only increased as the Ottoman government took out foreign loans to carry out much-needed reforms and public works. The commercial interests of the European powers severely limited the Ottoman economy while increasing their influence over it.

The War of 1877-1878

The peace between Russia and the Ottoman Empire lasted 21 years and only endured that long because of the solidarity of the great powers, but in 1870, Prussia and France were at war, and the concert of Europe was shattered. Prussia had defeated Austria four years before in an effort to unite all of Germany. Russia took advantage of the divide to declare it would no longer abide by the clauses of the Treaty of Paris that forbade it to maintain warships in the Black Sea and the great powers. Unable to enforce them, it was hastened to negotiate a new treaty at London, which, in 1871, abrogated the Black Sea articles while confirming the rights of the Sultan over the Dardanelles.

Then, in 1873, Russia, Germany, and Austria-Hungary (the Austrian Empire transformed into a dual monarchy in 1867) created the Three Emperors League, the purpose of which was to preserve the peace by isolating France. The position of France and Britain as the Ottoman Empire's guarantors was, therefore, threatened. France now sought to actively undermine Ottoman sovereignty in the Balkans as a means of countering Russian and Austro-Hungarian influence in the region.

In fact, the Three Emperors League was always shaky over the Balkan question. Russia wanted to create a union of Slavic states (Serbia, Montenegro, Bosnia, and an independent Bulgaria) under its protection, while Austria-Hungary wanted to suppress all nationalist activity so as not to encourage it within its own dominions. The German Empire (established in 1871) wished to preserve the Ottoman Empire and avoid conflict between its partners. Thus, the awkward situation arose where Russia and France joined against the interests of Germany and Austria-Hungary, Russia's allies. Great Britain, not formally aligned with any of the other great powers, monitored the Balkans with anxiety.

The effects of Europe's new order were swiftly seen. In July 1875, a Serbian nationalist uprising began in the Ottoman province of Herzegovina, and by August, it had spilt over into Bosnia. The unrest spread throughout the Balkan Peninsula, largely in response to an economic downturn and oppressive treatment from Muslim landowners. The decision to permit Christian subjects to be conscripted into the Sultan's army also contributed to the unrest. The disquiet was not confined to Christians - ethnic Albanians, who were mostly Muslims, also rose against their masters. The flames of revolt did not burn as fiercely in Wallachia and Moldavia, for they were already self-governing, joined as the United Principalities of Moldavia and Wallachia, but even so, they were aware of an opportunity to declare their absolute independence if Russia intervened. Serbia had also been effectively independent for many years, but its prince, MIlian Obrevonic IV, was mindful of Austria-Hungary's strong presence and refused to applaud the Serb risings in Herzegovina and Bosnia.

The sultan at the time was Abdul-Aziz, who came to the throne in 1861. He was a grand moderniser and ambitious for his empire but at a colossal cost. He believed that the key to diplomatic independence was a large navy, so he built one that was the third largest in the world after Great Britain and France, but this and other achievements required huge foreign loans, mostly from Britain and France, which could not be paid back. On October 30, 1875, his government declared a sovereign default and increased taxes to address the demands of its creditors. This had a catastrophic effect on the populace, particularly in the Balkans, and exacerbated an already volatile situation. On April 20, 1876, an organized revolt broke out in Bulgaria, which until that time, had not been granted any degree of autonomy. The Ottoman government responded by sending in *bashi-bazouks*, irregular soldiers who lived largely off of loot and perpetrated numerous atrocities. Thousands of civilians were massacred without pity, and the Bulgarian uprising was effectively quashed toward the end of May 1876.

Reports of the killings quickly reached the foreign embassies in Constantinople, and from there to the newspapers of the world. Not trusting the pro-Ottoman British, the Bulgarian community in Constantinople asked the United States consul, Eugene Schuyler, to go to Bulgaria to make a report. In November 1876, he reported that 58 villages and five monasteries had been destroyed, and 15,000 had been killed. Bulgarian commentators claimed the number of victims was double that figure,[20] while modern historians generally estimate that as many as 100,000 may have perished.[21]

Schuyler's report was widely published and drew general condemnation in Europe. In Great Britain, Leader of the Opposition William Gladstone attacked Benjamin Disraeli's government for its apparent indifference to the plight of Hungary and called for Bulgaria's freedom. In this, he was generally supported by the public, leaving Gladstone with the awkward task of attempting to preserve the Sultan and his own government. Russia expressed the most vehement outrage, for the Bulgarians were fellow Slavs, and most of them were Orthodox Christians.

By the time the storm of almost universal protest arrived at the door of the Sultan's palace,

---

[20] Jelavich, 1999, pp. 347
[21] Jelavich and Jelavich, 1977, p. 139

Abdul-Aziz was gone. On May 30, the Ottoman cabinet, in agreement with the military and chief Muslim clerics, deposed him for economic mismanagement and extravagance. A scapegoat had to be found to head off a full-scale revolution, though the Bulgarian atrocities were not mentioned in the statement of deposition. His nephew was called to the throne as Murad V, and four days later, Abdul-Aziz's bloodied corpse was discovered in his private apartments.

It was hoped that Murad would introduce a constitution and parliament, but he was mentally ill and unable to deal with the crisis facing the empire. He reigned for only 93 days before being deposed and replaced by his brother, Abdul Hamid II.

On June 30, 1876, the Principality of Serbia, nominally an Ottoman vassal, declared war and was joined by the Principality of Montenegro, which had long enjoyed independence from Constantinople. Russian Tsar Alexander II wished to intervene but needed to consult with Austria-Hungary. In their discussions - not confirmed by a published treaty - Russia and Austria-Hungary redrew the map of the Balkans, and pursuant to those discussions, Austria-Hungary was to occupy Bosnia and Herzegovina to prevent those provinces from becoming a part of a greater Serbia. Russia would receive southern Bessarabia (lost at the end of the Crimean War), and Bulgaria would become an autonomous principality. The agreement gave no support to Serbia, which was suffering a string of defeats, and so the Serbs asked the great powers to mediate in September 1876. The powers forced a truce on the Ottoman government, but peace talks failed, and when the truce expired in early October, the Ottoman Empire resumed its offensive.

The diplomatic situation escalated when, on October 31, Russia partially mobilised and demanded the Ottomans agree to a new truce within 48 hours. On December 11, a conference of the great powers (now including Italy) met at Constantinople. The fact that the Ottoman delegates were excluded from the working sessions showed the measure of disdain with which the empire was regarded by all the powers, and all the Ottoman government's proposals were rejected. The Ottoman government tried to head off a hostile decision by announcing that Sultan Abdul Hamid II had approved a constitution and a parliament, but this proved useless. On December 23, the representatives of the powers agreed to a settlement based on the July agreement between Austria-Hungary and Russia. Bosnia and Herzegovina would become an autonomous province under Austro-Hungarian protection, and Bulgaria was to be divided into two provinces, east and west, with substantial autonomy.

The powers did not confine themselves to broad guidelines concerning the Balkans but dictated domestic policy concerning taxation, law and order, and constitutional and local government. Their high-handedness outraged the Ottomans, and on January 18, 1877, Abdul Hamid rejected the conference's demands. By that time, Russia had already determined to go to war and had secured Austria-Hungary's neutrality.

Tsar Alexander II declared war on April 24, 1877 with Russian troops already in the United Principalities with the permission of their prince, Carol I, and Ottoman batteries immediately shelled Romanian towns on the Danube.

Militarily, the Ottoman Empire was in a more advantageous position than during the Crimean War. To begin with, it had complete command of the Black Sea, and although the 1871 London treaty had allowed Russia to rebuild its navy there, it was no match for the third-largest navy in the world. Ottoman gunships patrolled the Danube, and 200,000 troops were deployed in the Balkans. It was true that the Russians outnumbered them by about 100,000, but the Ottomans, perhaps for the first time in their conflicts with the Russians, possessed superior British and American-made rifles and artillery. On the other hand, about half of the Ottoman army was committed to fortifications and had to rely on a defensive strategy, which surrendered the initiative to the Russians.

The first objective of the Russians and Romanians was to free the Danube for their troops to cross. After a Romanian torpedo boat successfully destroyed an Ottoman monitor (small-armored steamship), the main invasion force crossed at Shvistov at the end of June. The Danubian fortress of Nicopolis (Nikopol) was captured soon after, and that had a huge effect on morale, for the Ottomans had defeated a crusader army that aimed to liberate Bulgaria near the area in 1396. A force under Grand Duke Nicholas of Russia then marched about 60 miles southwest and attacked the fortress of Plevna. This was defended by Field Marshal Osman Nuri Pasha, who ably repelled two assaults and forced the Grand Duke to call for Romanian reinforcements and begin a long siege. The Ottomans only surrendered after 145 days, and though the fall of the citadel was a blow, it delayed the progress of the Russian Army toward Constantinople.

While a part of the invading army was held up at Plevna, another force, joined by Bulgarian volunteers, assaulted the Shipka Pass, a vital passage through the Balkan Mountains. This involved four battles between July 1877 and January 1878 and engaged around 70,000 men on both sides. The final assault on January 5-9 produced a crushing Ottoman defeat and dispelled the last hope of relieving Plevna and fighting the Russians to a stalemate. Another Russian force drove toward Sofia and captured that city after defeating the Ottomans at the Battle of Tashkessen on December 31.

Meanwhile, the Principality of Serbia declared war on the Ottomans on December 13, 1877, and though restrained by Austro-Hungary, the Serbians made progress against positions on the Morava River in Rumelia (now southern Serbia). On the Caucasian front, Russian troops under Grand Duke Michael captured Kars on November 18, and by the end of February 1878, after a long siege, he was at Erzurum.

After the capture of Shipka Pass and the fall of Sofia Russian, Romanian and Bulgarian troops took Plovdiv and converged on Adrianople (Edirne), where the Ottomans made their last spirited resistance in February. The city fell, leaving no significant resistance between Adrianople and Constantinople, less than 200 miles to the east. The Ottoman government sued for peace, and on

January 31, the Russians agreed to an armistice, though they continued toward Constantinople. On February 2, Greece declared war on the Ottoman Empire and sent 10,000 troops into Thessaly.

Austria-Hungary, Britain, France, Germany, and Italy were all concerned. They had dared not intervene during the conflict for fear of escalating a general European war, but now they saw that Russia was going to dictate a peace that would make it master of the Balkans. The British, in particular, were fearful that Russian troops would occupy Constantinople, so they sent a fleet to Constantinople as a warning. The situation further escalated when, on February 15, Russia pressured Abdul Hamid II to forbid the British entrance, but the fleet appeared before the Ottoman capital nevertheless. On March 3, the Russian army halted at San Stefano (Yeşilköy), a day's march short of the capital, and imposed peace terms. The Treaty of Stan Stefano made Bulgaria a self-governing state, subject to Constantinople in a purely nominal manner. It would maintain its own army and a constitution and a prince elected by the people. Its territory would include Macedonia and Eastern Thrace. Romania, Serbia, and Montenegro would receive territory and be granted formal independence, and several other territories, including Thessaly and Greece, would receive a measure of self-government.

Thus, despite the other Europeans' concerns, the Russian Empire had successfully imposed a peace that effectively seemed to create a Pan-Slavic empire in the Balkans. Great Britain could not tolerate Bulgarian territory so close to Constantinople, while Austria-Hungary viewed the Treaty of San Stefano as a betrayal of pre-war agreements with Russia concerning Bosnia and Herzegovina. The German Empire saw the treaty as potentially breaking up the Three Emperors League, thus endangering its status in Europe. As for France, it had little direct interest in the region, though destabilizing the triple alliance was fine with the French since it adversely affected Germany.

The powers agreed to meet in Berlin for talks on June 13, 1878. The Congress of Berlin met under the threat of war, for Britain had already made an alliance with the Ottoman Empire and agreed to hand over Bosnia-Herzegovina to Austria-Hungary in return for support against Russia. It seemed that talks might fail and be replaced by war, but Chancellor Bismarck succeeded in persuading the other delegates to adopt a compromise settlement. Bulgaria would be divided, with the north becoming an autonomous principality and the south (Eastern Rumelia) remaining with the Ottoman Empire. Bulgaria would lose Macedonia, thus placating Britain, which did not want Russia having a friendly port in the Mediterranean. Romania and Serbia would gain their independence and be enlarged, along with Montenegro. Bosnia and Herzegovina would remain a part of the Ottoman Empire but would be administered by Austria-Hungary.

Peace had been achieved, but as with many other peace deals of its kind, it only ensured future wars.

Prelude to World War I

The Congress of Berlin did not, of course, settle the eastern question. It was a pragmatic agreement made to avoid war and preserve the Three Emperors League. The Russian Empire, which had come so close to controlling Constantinople, the goal of over 150 years of diplomacy and conflict, was now forced to pull back within sight of the Ottoman capital's minarets. Russian society generally resented that Holy Mother Russia had been thwarted in the fulfilment of her destiny.

The Ottomans also had cause to feel they had been betrayed by Western powers, which had promised to guarantee its borders before the war. Now, they had been forced to consent to the piecemeal disintegration of the empire. The Ottoman government knew all too well that once independence had been granted to the Romanians and Serbs and self-government was granted to the Bulgarians; the divided powers would struggle to deny liberation to Slavs and Greeks still under Ottoman rule. Indeed, only three years after the Treaty of Berlin, the empire was compelled to cede Thessaly to Greece.

After the Russian War, Abdul Hamid II suspended the Ottoman Constitution and dissolved the parliament, which had only met once. Without turning his back on the modernisation of the empire, he denounced the liberalisation of the government as a contributing factor to its decline.

He would rule personally until his deposition in 1908. During his reign, the humiliating Ottoman Public Debt Administration was established at the insistence of the great powers, founded in 1881 to garner revenue to pay to European creditors. The governors of the authority were mostly representatives of foreign governments, making the Ottoman Empire an economic colony, in essence, and severely hampering its development. This fact was highlighted by the 1882 occupation of Egypt by Britain to protect its interests there.

Another bitter humiliation came in 1885 when, on September 26, the Principality of Bulgaria annexed Eastern Rumelia in violation of the Treaty of Berlin. The Ottoman Empire and Russia were restrained, and the honour of the Berlin Congress was maintained by the fiction that Bulgaria remained divided, except that Prince Alexander of Bulgaria was now also the governor-general of Eastern Rumelia. The invention fooled no-one and only served to highlight the weakness of the Berlin settlement.

The uneasy peace in the Balkans was again endangered when a young Emperor Wilhelm II of Germany dismissed Chancellor Bismarck and abandoned the relationship with Russia. The Russian Empire responded by seeking an alliance with France. The understanding between the three empires over the Balkans, tenuous as it was, was thereby broken, and Russia felt as if it had a freer hand. War threatened to break out over the Balkans when, on October 5, 1908, the

Principality of Bulgaria declared itself independent. On the following day, Franz Josef I of Austria-Hungary declared the formal annexation of Bosnia and Herzegovina.

These twin actions set off a series of escalating events. Serbia protested the seizure of ethnically Serbian lands it desired for itself, and Great Britain called the annexation of Bosnia and Herzegovina a violation of the Treaty of Berlin. Then, on July 24, leaders of a reform movement calling themselves the Young Turks staged a coup against Abdul Hamid II, forcing him to restore the constitution and parliament. The new government refused to recognise the independence of Bulgaria but had no policy on how to deal with it. Meanwhile, Russia expressed support for Bulgaria and Serbia, and war was only narrowly avoided when Germany backed Austria-Hungary and forced Russia to stand down. Ironically, the Russian Empire had already experienced its own revolution in 1905 over a failure to modernise. Its defeat in the 1904-1905 Russo-Japanese War triggered an uprising, and the imperial government promised to call a popularly-elected *Duma,* or parliament. Both the Russian and Ottoman Empires struggled to reform, the difference being that the introduction of a liberalised regime in Turkey was, at least, sincere. Emperor Nicholas II had no intention of surrendering his autocratic powers to an elected assembly.

In October 1911, Italian soldiers, along with troops from the Italian Somaliland and Eritrea, landed in Tripolitania in present day Libya. Italy's claim over the last Ottoman province in North Africa stemmed from verbal agreements with France and England. The two leading powers of the time offered to balance the French protectorate over Tunisia and British control over Cyprus by creating an Italian colony in Libya. This agreement was not enforced until 1911, when Italy felt threatened by the growing French expansionism in North Africa, which could see the western Mediterranean becoming a "French Lake." Libya was also seen as a door to sub-Saharan Africa and a potential commercial hub.

The invasion itself was short. While the Ottoman army managed to launch a successful counter-offensive led by Mustafa Kemal against Italian troops in Tobruk, it was rapidly overwhelmed when Italy sent further reinforcements. The modernization of the Ottoman army wasn't complete at the time, particularly within the Ottoman Navy, which still relied mostly on wooden ships. The Italian military employed modern military equipment and would carry out the first airstrikes in military history during the campaign. In October 1912, the Ottoman army was defeated, and a treaty was signed asserting Italian control over Libya, despite the fact that the invasion triggered a significant Arab rebellion against the Ottomans.

The swift defeat of the Ottoman military convinced the Balkan nations that the empire was finished, and Greece, Bulgaria, Serbia and Montenegro had been waiting for a chance to seize the remaining Ottoman possessions in Europe. The weakening of the Ottoman influence in its last European stronghold was further illustrated by the Albanian revolts of 1910 and 1912, which saw a Muslim population turn against the Young Turks. While the Ottoman army was still deployed in Libya, in October 1912 they all declared war on the Ottoman Empire. The Ottoman army, weakened by the war with Italy, was defeated by the coalition of Balkan nations. Salonika, the heart of the Young Turks' revolution, was occupied, along with Edirne, just west of Istanbul.

While the Ottomans had a chance to recapture Edirne as the former allies started turning against each other, the war had changed the Young Turks. The idea that fraternity amongst the communities forming the Empire could eventually save it was brushed aside by nationalistic realities. In the provinces freed by the Balkan coalition, emerging nations were waging war against each other, leading to the displacement of thousands of Muslims. The borders created by the conflict were unstable. For instance, the heart of the Albanian revolt, Kosovo, was given to Serbia. As a result of the defeat, the Young Turks grew more nationalistic, putting an emphasis on the Turkish identity, and ethnic homogeneity. Beyond that, the feeling that the Ottoman Empire was being dismantled by their so-called allies, namely France and England, as well as changes within the Young Turks, sealed the Ottomans' alliance with Germany.

The Ottomans' relations with Germany were not new. In the same way that France sought the support of the Sublime Porte in its fight against central European powers during the 16th century, Germany saw the Ottoman Empire as a possible strategic partner against Russia, France, and England. German Kaiser Wilhelm II visited the Ottoman Empire on two occasions before World War I and sought to encourage Abdul Hamid's pan-Islamism, which he saw as a useful tool against the British colonialism. During his second visit in 1898, the Kaiser visited the tomb of Saladin in Damascus and offered to pay for its renovation. Arab newspapers praised the visit, stating that the Kaiser was "the best friend of the great Sultan;" and "the most sincere and loyal monarch in his friendship toward the Sultan." The German Emperor even earned the title of "Hajji Wilhelm."

Wilhelm II

Economic relations expanded with the building of the Baghdad Railway, starting in 1903. The Prussian and later German military expertise was also increasingly used by the Ottoman army, peaking with the German mission of 1913, led by German military officer Otto Liman von Sanders.

Despite that, the Ottoman Empire did not initially seek to formally ally with Germany, much less participate in a global conflict. In fact, as the 1910s dawned, the growing rivalry between the Entente alliance (France, Russia, and Britain)[22] and the Central Powers (the Austro-Hungarian Empire and Germany), seemed like a distant problem. Ironically, the Ottoman Empire sought on multiple occasions to enter into an alliance with the British, French and Russians, or to at least

____

[22] Referring to the Triple Entente, an agreement between these three powers signed in the wake of the "Entente Cordiale" (Cordial Friendship) treaty between France and England in 1904 and the Anglo-Russian Entente of 1907.

secure an agreement regarding its neutrality during a potential conflict. The alliance with Russia was, however, more central to the British and French, who refused the various Ottoman proposals.

The disastrous war against the Balkan states brought together the changes needed to convince the Ottomans of the benefit of the alliance with the Kaiser. As the war broke out, Enver Pasha[23] (Ismail Enver) returned from Libya to Istanbul on January 1913. Three days after his arrival, he participated in a coup against the Turkish government led by the CUP's rival, the LU. Together with Talaat Pasha and Djemal Pasha, they formed a dictatorial triumvirate dubbed the "Three Pashas." Enver played a critical role in the empire's entry into the coming war on the side of Germany; he had been the Empire's military attaché and was convinced that a military alliance with the Germany would be beneficial.

Enver's conviction stemmed from his perception of the Kaiser's military strength, as well as the understanding that while the Entente did not need the Ottomans to win the war, Germany did, and the Germans would thus act to strengthen the Ottomans. He also represented the military officers among the Young Turks who admired the Prussian state and the central role played by the army in the building of the German nation. Finally, his decision to back an alliance with Germany stemmed from the belief that the upcoming war between the European nations would be a short one that could present opportunities to counter-balance the Ottomans' territorial losses at the expense of Russia and England.

Nonetheless, he was the only one among the Three Pashas to believe in the German-Ottoman alliance. Both Djemal and Talaat Pasha favored an alliance with the Entente, while Sultan Mehmed V supported the empire's neutrality. The Ottomans' pledge for an alliance with the British failed in 1913, along with a later request made by Talaat Pasha to Russia and another one to France made by Djemal Pasha. Enver swayed Djemal Pasha, and on July 22, 1914, six days before the official beginning of World War I, the Ottomans officially offered the signing of an alliance with Germany.

Despite the initial reluctance of the German foreign office, which feared the Ottomans' weakness would be a burden, the Kaiser pushed for an alliance that he saw as a way to divert forces from other critical fronts. On August 2, the secret alliance between the Ottoman Empire and Germany, an alliance that would be fatal to the old empire, was signed. In the wake of the agreement, on October 29, the Ottoman fleet, reinforced by two German naval ships, carried out a surprise attack on the Russian Black Sea fleet, prompting a declaration of war by the Entente powers.

The Legacy of the Ottoman-Russian Wars

When World War I began, the Ottoman Empire was still neutral and the cabinet divided,

---

[23] Pasha is an honorary title given, originally, to military commanders.

though Enver Pasha, now minister of war, was fiercely pro-German and allowed German war vessels to pass through the Straits in violation of international law. Still, the empire declared its neutrality. Then, on September 14, Enver Pasha ordered a raid on Russian ports without the knowledge of the cabinet or the consent of the minister of the navy. It proved a fateful decision. The government attempted to explain and protest its neutrality, but it was too late, and Russia declared war on November 5, 1914.

During World War I, the Ottoman Empire fought a multi-pronged war that would greatly strain its resources, leading to starvation and great suffering for the local populations. In the east, the Russians opened the war with an offensive in the Caucasus a few days after the Ottomans' surprise attack. This front would be one of the toughest in the war, not only because of the Russian human resources but also because of the climate and strategic mistakes by the Ottoman military leadership. Enver Pasha, the Ottoman Minister of War, was hoping that a swift victory against Russia would lay the groundwork for Turkey's expansion in the Caucasus and a revolt of local Muslim populations. In this, Enver was guided by his "Pan-Turkism," which sought to create a Turkish region in the Caucasus.

As the Russian offensive began, Enver ordered the launching of a complex attack against the Russian forces, disregarding the opinion of General Hasan Izzet Pasha, the commander of the Third Army based in eastern Turkey. In December, as the front stabilized despite the initial failed offensive, Enver sent one of his emissaries to Izzet Pasha, ordering a planned spring offensive on Sarikamis to be launched immediately. Enver believed that with superior numbers (the Ottomans had a force of more than 110,000 men while the Russians only had 65,000) the Turkish force would be able to swiftly encircle and destroy the Russian army. The Ottoman army, however, was ill-equipped, poorly trained and lacked the proper experience of mountain warfare to carry on such a complex operation.

Izzet

Faced with Izzet Pasha's reluctance to launch such a risky operation in a mountainous area during the winter, Enver left Istanbul to take personal command of the offensive. After a failed assault on Russian positions, the Ottoman army withdrew to regroup and launch a new attempt. During the march, the cold, mountainous terrain and exhaustion of the Ottoman troops resulted in devastating casualties. The 10th Corps, for instance, lost 90% of its soldiers in what came to be called the "Death March."

Enver's Sarikamis offensive ended in a disaster. Epidemics and a renewed Russian offensive deepened the blow the following year. This disaster was rapidly blamed on the Armenians, who had supposedly betrayed the Ottoman Empire. In April 1915, Armenian intellectuals in Istanbul were executed, paving the way for the first large-scale genocide in modern history. Russian advances would only be stopped by the Bolshevik Revolution in 1917, which took Russia out of the war entirely.

In Mesopotamia,[24] a British force mostly made of Indian soldiers from the British Empire launched an offensive in the south in November 1914, by first taking Basra. While the British initially only sought to protect their oil interests, including the nearby complex of Abadan, the swift capture of Basra convinced them of the benefits of a campaign in Mesopotamia. The

---

[24] Present-day Iraq.

British force was ordered to march towards Kut, north of Basra. Understanding the threat posed by the offensive, Enver Pasha sent reinforcements to Baghdad and ordered the launch of a counter-offensive to retake the Shatt al-Arab.[25] The local Ottoman commander, instead, waged a successful but costly defensive war, leading to the initial surrender of the British force under Major General Charles Townshend. The British, however, sent a new commander, General Stanley Maude, along with reinforcements and ordered the expansion of the port of Basra, leading to a new offensive against Kut. The offensive was successful, opening the way for the capture of Baghdad in 1916 and an offensive in the Anbar province in 1917-18.

Maude

Meanwhile, in the west, close to Istanbul, the Entente's inability to carry out a naval siege of the capital led to the sending of a French and British expeditionary force that landed on the mainland in April 1915. The Ottomans knew the Dardanelles strait would most certainly be attacked and had prepared significant defenses. The plan drafted by the then First Lord of the

---

[25] The confluence of the Euphrates and Tigris.

Admiralty, Winston Churchill, was meant to destroy Ottoman defenses along the Dardanelles. However, allied forces made of British, Irish, Australian and New Zealanders were unable to penetrate the Ottoman defenses, advancing only about 100 meters from the shores. The Ottomans, led by German General Liman von Sanders, further reinforced their positions. The later attempt of the British to establish a new beachhead was more successful, yet the British government refused to send significant reinforcements.

The first of the empires to fall was Russia in February 1917. Tsar Nicholas II abdicated and was later murdered with his family by the Bolsheviks. On October 30 of the following year, Sultan Mehmed VI surrendered, and in 1922, the Sultanate was abolished. Both empires collapsed because they failed to make the reforms needed to survive. The changes they made were directed largely toward each other, and perhaps it is not too much of an exaggeration to say their mutual enmity ultimately consumed and destroyed them.

The fall of the Ottoman Empire set the political and geostrategic scene of the new Middle East. In 1920, two years after the end of the war, the region was already experiencing growing instability. The issues and trends that would plague the region until today were growing. On April 4, Arab riots broke out in Jerusalem, fueled by the growing hostility against the Zionist movement. The British passivity would convince one of the Jewish leaders, Vladimir Jabotinsky (the future founder of the Israeli right-wing), of the strategic necessity of a strong Jewish military as the core of the future state.

Jabotinsky

Just two weeks later in Turkey, the Grand National Assembly in Ankara set the foundation of the Turkish state, opening the way for 8 years of reforms. In Iraq, a Shiite revolt broke out in the south, as locals demanded the creation of an Islamic state. The British compromise was to place Faisal, the son of Sharif Hussein and a Sunni, on the throne. His father, meanwhile, was embroiled in a conflict with a local tribe, the Ibn Saud, that sought to carve a new kingdom in the Arabian Peninsula.

More broadly, the long decline of the "sick man of Europe" fostered the emergence of nationalistic and ideological movements that are still key to any understanding of the Middle East today. The compatibility between the Islamic religion and culture and Western reforms were first discussed within the Empire, and they are still up for debate today. Abdul Hamid's pan-Islamism, while its results at the time remain limited, still resonates within the Muslim world and can still be seen as a viable rival to the region's various nationalistic aspirations.

In fact, almost 100 years after the fall of the Ottoman Empire, it is clear that the emergence of secular Arab nationalism triggered an opposite reaction from supporters of a political Islam and vice versa. The Muslim Brotherhood, for instance, was created as a reaction to the abolition of the Caliphate by Turkey in 1928 and would strengthen its ranks by being a viable opponent to the rising secular Arab nationalism. These mechanics are still at work today, as an initial wave of secular revolutions, the Arab Spring, triggered a second wave of "Green Revolutions." In parallel, whether in its most radical form with ISIS and al-Qaeda's idea of a Caliphate, or in the moderate ideology with the emergence of political Islam, Islam is still seen as an effective weapon against Western influence. In Turkey itself, the opposition between partisans of a strong Islamic identity and those such as Mustafa Kemal, who rejected it, still divides the political and social landscape.

These challenges, divides, and conflicts all stem from the power vacuum slowly left by the once powerful Ottoman Empire, and the issue of the Dardanelle Straits is still a sore subject between Russia and Turkey. The former still relies on freedom of navigation through them for its economy, and although Russia and Turkey have not been at war for over 100 years, the issue continues to shape the region. The annexation of Crimea in 2014, for example, was done largely to secure Russia's access to the Black Sea, and the tensions between the two nations in the Middle East and the Caucasus have as much to do with economic domination as any other factor. Turkey's membership in NATO and its ties with the European Union, tenuous as they might be, also concerns the Russian Federation.

Online Resources

Other books about Russian history by Charles River Editors

Other books about Middle East history by Charles River Editors

Other books about the Ottomans on Amazon

Further Reading

Baumgart Winifred. (2020). *The Crimean War: 1853-1856,* Bloomsbury Publishing.

Ben-Zaken, Avner. (2010). *Cross-Cultural Scientific Exchanges in the Eastern Mediterranean, 1560–1660* (2010).

Billy, André. (1937). *La Grèce*, Arthaud.

Brewer, David. (2011). *The Greek War of Independence*, Overlook Duckworth.

Burckhardt, C. J. (1947). *Richelieu* vol. 2 (English edition 1970).

Chandler, David G. (1980). *Atlas of Military Strategy*, Lionel Levental Ltd.

Clodfelter, M. (2017). *Warfare and Armed Conflicts: A Statistical Encyclopedia of Casualty and Other Figures, 1492-2015* (4th ed.), McFarland.

Daskalov, Roumen and Tchavdar Marinov. (2013). *Entangled Histories of the Balkans - Volume One: National Ideologies and Language Policies,* BRILL.

Jelavich, Barbara. (1999). *History of the Balkans: Eighteenth and Nineteenth Centuries, Nide 1,* Cambridge University Press.

Jelavich, Charles and Barbara Jelavich. (1977). *The Establishment of the Balkan National States, 1804–1920,* University of Washington Press.

Kent, Marian. (1996). *The Great Powers and the End of the Ottoman Empire,* Routledge.

Kinross, Lord. (1977). *The Ottoman Centuries: The Rise and Fall of the Turkish Empire,* William Morrow and Company, Inc.

Maule, Fox *(1908/2009). The Panmure Papers,* quoted in David Kelsey's Crimean Texts, *Hodder and Stoughton.*

Reynolds, Michael A. (2011). *Shattering Empires: The Clash and Collapse of the Ottoman and Russian Empires 1908–1918,* Cambridge University Press.

Royle, Trevor (2000). *Crimea: The Great Crimean War, 1854–1856.* Palgrave Macmillan.

Schwarzenbach, R. (1978). *Schweizerisches Archiv für Volksunde* 74.

Free Books by Charles River Editors

We have brand new titles available for free most days of the week. To see which of our titles are currently free, click on this link.

Discounted Books by Charles River Editors

We have titles at a discount price of just 99 cents everyday. To see which of our titles are currently 99 cents, <u>click on this link</u>.